$$\cos x = \frac{A}{H}$$

$$\frac{O}{A}$$

$$\frac{1}{2} \times \frac{3}{4} = \frac{3}{8}$$

c^2

a^2

b^2

AIR
SCIENCE
TRICKS

Library of Congress Cataloging-in-Publication Data

Murray, Peter, 1952 Sept. 29
    Professor Solomon Snickerdoodle's Air Science Tricks / author, Peter Murray:
Penny Dann, illustrator.
    p. cm.
    ISBN 1-56766-082-7
    1. Air—Juvenile literature. 2. Air—Experiments—Juvenile literature. [1. Air—
Experiments. 2. Experiments.] I. Title. II. Title: Air science tricks.
QC161.2.M88 1998
533'.6'078—DC20   98-7608

                                            CIP
                                            AC

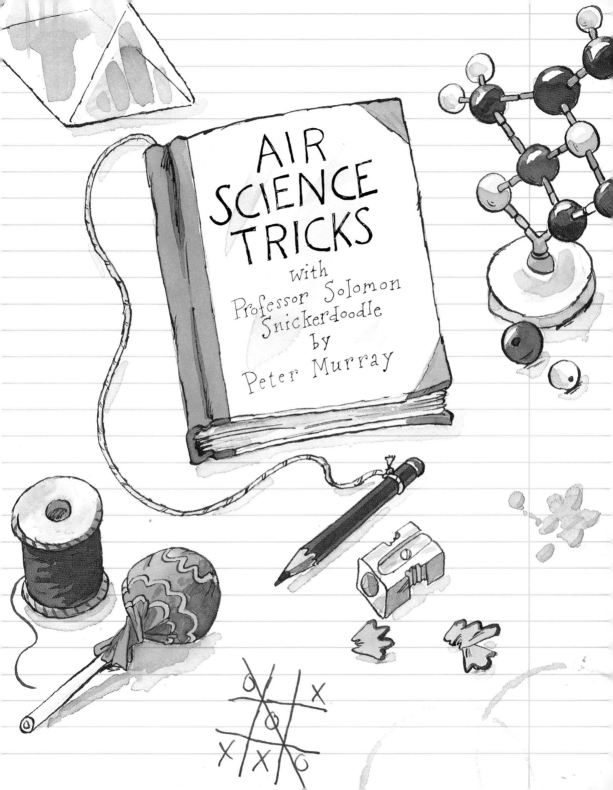

BANG!

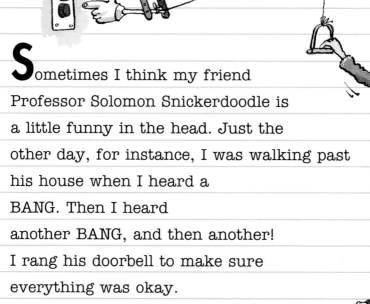

Sometimes I think my friend
Professor Solomon Snickerdoodle is
a little funny in the head. Just the
other day, for instance, I was walking past
his house when I heard a
BANG. Then I heard
another BANG, and then another!
I rang his doorbell to make sure
everything was okay.

When the door opened, he was
standing there with his topknot in an uproar. He was
holding a big red balloon in one hand. His mechanical
dog looked worried.

"Good afternoon,
Professor," I said.

The professor said, "It's
incontestable,
incontrovertible,
and superlative! Air expands!"

Lately, the professor has been using a lot of big words. He thinks it makes him sound smart, but sometimes I think he doesn't know what he's saying.

Suddenly another BANG came from inside the house. The dog and I both J U M P E D !

"What was that!!!?" I asked.

"That," said the professor with a grin, "was the sound of air expanding! Come into my laboratory, my young friend!"

I knew then that the professor was going to show me one of his remarkable experiments.

THE TIME BOMB BALLOONS

The professor showed me the balloon in his hand and asked, "What do you notice about this balloon?"

"It's red," I said.

"Please be more specific!" he said, frowning in a professorish way.

I held the balloon. "Well," I said, "It's blown up *really* tight. Another puff of air and I'll bet it would pop!" What else can you say about a red balloon?

"Indisputably!" cried the professor. He took the balloon and set it on a radiator. I noticed several pieces of exploded balloon lying on the floor near the radiator.

That explained the "bangs" I had heard! But what had made the balloons explode?

I looked at the red balloon. Nothing was happening.

"Now we wait," said the professor, covering his ears.

So we waited, hands over our ears, for what seemed like a very long time. After a while, I started to think that the experiment was a failure. I took my hands off my ears and went into the kitchen to look for a cookie.

Wouldn't you know it! As soon as I forgot about the balloon, it went **BANG!**

HOW TO MAKE A TIME BOMB BALLOON:

1. Blow up a balloon as tight as you can. It has to be very, very tight for this experiment to work! Use a balloon pump if you have one, or find an adult with strong lungs to help you. Tie off the balloon.

2. Put the balloon in a warm place. You can set it on a radiator, tie it to a heat vent, set it on top of a lamp (not too close to the bulb, though!) or put it in a hot, sunny window.

3. Wait. Sometimes you only have to wait a few minutes. Sometimes you have to wait for hours—and sometimes the balloons never blow up at all. With Time Bomb Balloons, you never know for sure!

REMEMBER

Remember, the balloon must be blown up very tight, and you must put it in a very warm place. If it doesn't work at first, don't give up! Just when you least expect it . . .

KA-BLAM!

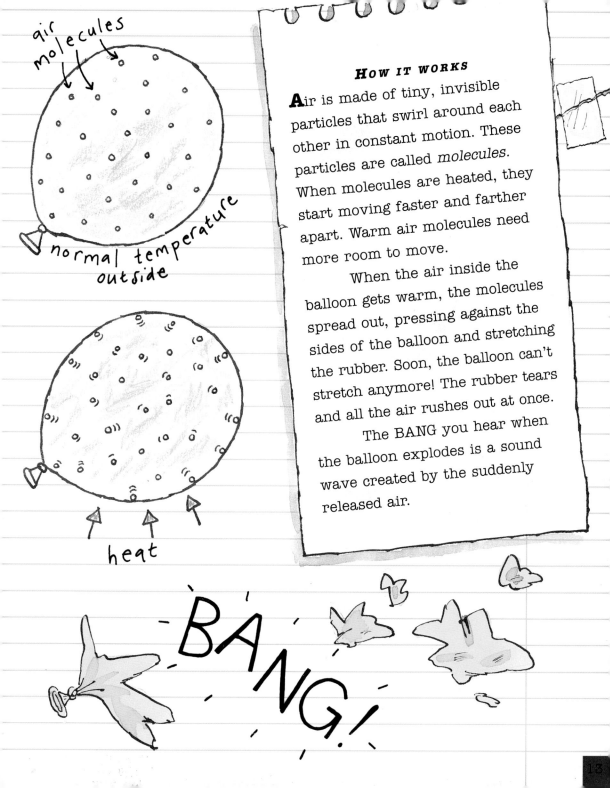

air molecules

normal temperature outside

heat

HOW IT WORKS

Air is made of tiny, invisible particles that swirl around each other in constant motion. These particles are called *molecules*. When molecules are heated, they start moving faster and farther apart. Warm air molecules need more room to move.

When the air inside the balloon gets warm, the molecules spread out, pressing against the sides of the balloon and stretching the rubber. Soon, the balloon can't stretch anymore! The rubber tears and all the air rushes out at once.

The BANG you hear when the balloon explodes is a sound wave created by the suddenly released air.

BANG!

THE COLLAPSING POP BOTTLE

"**A**ir expands when it is heated," said the professor, "and contracts when it is cooled! Allow me to demonstrate."

The professor took a plastic bottle to his sink. He filled the bottle with water, waited a bit, then poured it out and screwed the top back on the empty bottle.

"Observe!" he commanded.

As we watched, the sides of the bottle crumpled.

HOW TO CRUSH A BOTTLE WITH AIR PRESSURE:

1. Fill a large plastic soda pop bottle with HOT tap water. Let the water sit in the bottle for one minute to warm the plastic.

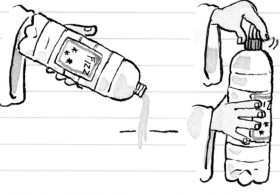

2. Pour out the hot water. As soon as the bottle is empty, quickly screw the cap on the bottle. Screw it on tight!

3. Now watch as the bottle **COLLAPSES!** You can speed up the process by running cold water over the outside of the empty bottle.

HOW IT WORKS

When you pour out the hot water, the air that rushes into the bottle is warmed by the hot plastic. The bottle cap traps the hot air in the bottle. The hot air molecules are moving quickly, pressing out against the sides.

As the air inside the bottle cools, the molecules slow and the air pressure inside the bottle decreases. But the air pressure *outside* remains constant, pressing hard on the outside of the bottle, causing it to collapse!

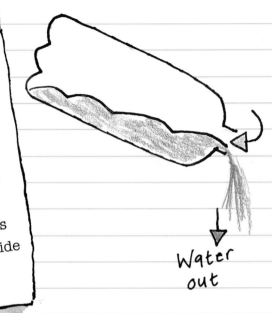

Water out

Warmed air molecules spread out and whizz around, pressing against the sides of the bottle.

Cooler air molecules press against the sides less than those inside the bottle.

The air inside cools, and the molecules stop pushing out against the sides so much.

The air molecules outside are now pressing in much more than those in the bottle are pushing out and....

"That's pretty cool, Professor," I said. "But how do you know the air is doing it? It looks to me like the plastic is crinkling all on its own."

The professor looked hurt.

"You doubt my word? Then let me show you one of my favorite experiments. . . ."

THE AMAZING INDEX CARD

The professor filled a glass with water. Then he put an index card over the top of the glass. Holding the card in place, he turned the glass upside down and let go of the card.

I expected the water to spill all over his shoes, but nothing happened! The card stayed stuck to the rim, and the water stayed inside the glass!

How to make an Amazing Index Card:

All you need is a glass with a smooth rim, an index card (or some other piece of stiff, thin cardboard), and water.

1. Fill the glass with water.

2. Cover the top with the index card. Hold the card against the rim with one hand while you turn the glass upside down.

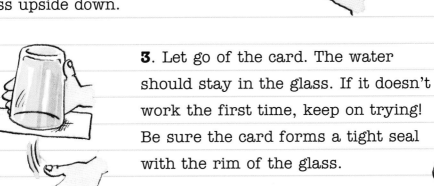

3. Let go of the card. The water should stay in the glass. If it doesn't work the first time, keep on trying! Be sure the card forms a tight seal with the rim of the glass.

Do this experiment over a sink or bathtub!

HOW IT WORKS:

Did you know that tons of air is pressing in on your body right now? Can you feel it?

The reason you are not crushed by all this weight (like the soda pop bottle in the previous experiment) is because you have pressure inside your body, too. The pressure in your body is about the same as the pressure of the air, so they cancel each other out.

Air pressure is what keeps the card pressed tight against the rim of the glass. There is 14.7 pounds of air pressure on every square inch of card, enough to hold the card in place.

147 pounds

Pressure outside balances pressure inside

Water presses down   glass

card

higher pressure outside pushes the card up

"The weight of the air pressing up on the card is more than the weight of the water?" I asked.

"Indubitably!" said the professor.

"But I didn't think air weighed anything!"

"Everything," said the professor, "weighs something!"

THE BALLOON BALANCE

"**B**low up these balloons," said the professor. He handed me a blue balloon and a red balloon. "Blow them up so they are the same size."

I blew up the balloons while the professor set up his experiment.

HOW TO MAKE A BALLOON BALANCE:

1. Tie the two inflated balloons to the ends of a wooden dowel about 3 feet long. Big balloons work best for this experiment.

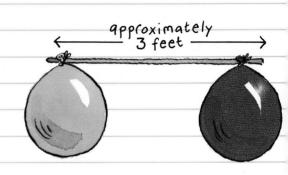

approximately 3 feet

2. Tie a string to the center of the dowel and hang it from a doorway or over the side of a table. Move the string on the dowel until you find the balancing point.

3. Let the air out of one of the balloons by carefully poking a pin or a sharp pencil very close to the knot. Don't just jab the balloon in the side or you'll have balloon all over the place! For this experiment, you want the balloon to stay in one piece. What happens?

"The balloon full of air weighs more than the balloon without air," I observed.

"Undoubtedly true," declared the professor. "Air has weight!"

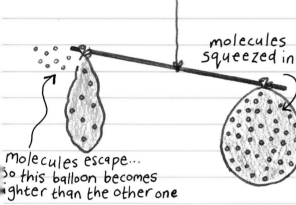

molecules squeezed in

molecules escape...
so this balloon becomes lighter than the other one

Something just didn't seem right to me. "If air is so heavy, how come people can go up in the air in balloons?" I asked.

"Hmmmm," said the professor. "That is a very provocative question!"

"Does that mean you don't know?" I asked.

"Don't be ridiculous!" the professor snapped.

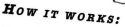

HOW IT WORKS:

When you first set up your Balloon Balance, each air-filled balloon appears to weigh the same. When you let the air out of one balloon, the other balloon goes down, showing that the air-filled balloon weighs more than the empty balloon.

The Balloon Balance experiment works because the air inside a balloon is under pressure. When you fill the balloon, you are squeezing the air with your lungs. This squeezes the air molecules closer together, making the air inside the balloon weigh more than the air outside the balloon. If the air in the balloon was not under so much pressure this experiment would not work.

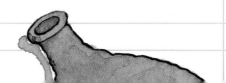

THE HOT AIR SNAKE

87
+42
———
129

The professor was babbling again. "As previously elucidated, everything weighs something, but some things weigh less than other things, and weighing less is more important than weight alone, relatively speaking. Do you understand?"

"No," I said. "You aren't making any sense!"

"That is because you are not listening," Snickerdoodle snapped. Sometimes the professor can be a little testy.

"I'm listening," I said, "but I think you're full of hot air!"

The professor's eyes bugged out. I thought he was about to pop like one of his balloons, but instead he exclaimed, "Hot air! That's it!"

The next thing I knew, Professor Snickerdoodle was making a Hot Air Snake!

HOW TO MAKE A HOT AIR SNAKE:

1. Draw a spiral on a sheet of paper. If you want to, you can decorate it. The middle of the spiral will be the snake's head.

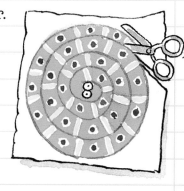

2. Cut out the spiral with scissors.

3. Poke a hole through the snake's head and run a string or thread through it. Tie a knot in one end of the string so that the snake hangs as shown.

4. Hold the snake above a radiator or a hot light bulb and watch it spin!

HOW IT WORKS:

Remember the way the air expanded when you put the Time Bomb Balloons in a warm place? The molecules in warm air are farther apart than the molecules in cool air. That means that warm air weighs less, so it rises. The warm air pushes up on the snake, causing it to spin!

The giant hot air balloons that carry people up into the sky work the same way. The air inside the balloon is heated. Soon, the air in the hot-air-filled balloon is much lighter than the air around it, and the balloon rises up into the sky.

$$\sin x = \frac{o}{H}$$

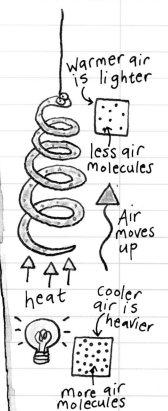

Warmer air is lighter

less air molecules

Air moves up

heat

Cooler air is heavier

more air molecules

THE BERNOULLI SPOOL

"Is that how airplanes fly?" I asked. "Are they full of hot air, too?"

"An entirely different thing altogether!" said the professor.

"Airplanes fly because of the Bernoulli Principle," explained Professor Snickerdoodle.

"Are you sure it isn't because they have wings?" I asked.

"Unequivocally! Airplane wings use the Bernoulli Principle!"

"I see," I said, although I did not see at all.

The professor continued. "In 1738, a Swiss scientist named Bernoulli discovered that moving air has less pressure than still air. The faster the air moves, the less air pressure it has. *That* is why airplanes fly!"

"So far," I said, "you have me completely *confuserized*."

The professor frowned.

"'Confuserized' is not a real word," he said.

"I don't get this Bernoulli stuff," I explained.

So the professor made a Bernoulli Spool.

HOW TO MAKE A BERNOULLI SPOOL:

1. You will need a spool of sewing thread (with or without the thread), a thumbtack, and an index card.

2. Push the thumbtack through the center of the card.

3. Place the end of the spool over the thumbtack and hold the card against the spool.

4. Blow through the spool and let go of the card. Blow as hard as you can. No matter how hard you blow, you can't blow the card away from the spool!

"Now do you understand?" asked the professor.

"No," I replied breathlessly.

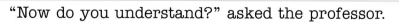

HOW IT WORKS:

The force that holds the card against the spool is the same force that helps airplanes fly. When you blow through the spool you create a stream of fast-moving air. This moving air has less pressure than the still air pressing on the back of the card. Air pressure keeps the card in place. The harder you blow, the more you decrease the pressure between the card and the spool.

Airplane wings use the same principle. The air passing over the curved top of the wing has to travel farther to get past the wing, so it must move faster than the air moving past the flat bottom. This means the air pressure on the bottom of the wing is greater. Air pushes the wing up, and the airplane flies!

Cross-section diagram

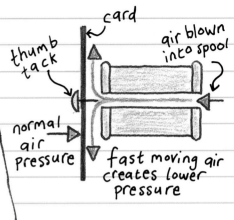

card

thumb tack

air blown into spool

normal air pressure

fast moving air creates lower pressure

A. this air has to travel faster to meet the air travelling underneath

AIR

WING

B. this situation creates **LIFT!**

lower pressure

WING

higher pressure

"So what do you think about air?" the professor asked.

"I think it's *fantabulous*," I said.

The professor stroked his chin and smiled.

"*Absotively*," he said.

$E = mc^2$

$a^2 + b^2 = c^2$

$\frac{1}{2}bh = \text{area of triangle}$

11
×5
55